STRUCTURED COUNSELING ACTIVITIES

FOR COUPLES, FAMILIES, AND INDIVIDUALS

CLYDE M. FELDMAN, PH.D.

i

A Clyde Feldman, Ph.D. Publication

STRUCTURED COUNSELING ACTIVITIES
FOR COUPLES, FAMILIES, AND INDIVIDUALS

Copyright © 2012, rev. 2021 Clyde M. Feldman, Ph.D.

All rights reserved.

Printed in the United States of America

*****

Formatting By Debora Lewis
www.arenapublishing.org

ISBN-13: 978-1480063129

ISBN-10: 1480063126

STRUCTURED COUNSELING ACTIVITIES
FOR COUPLES, FAMILIES, AND INDIVIDUALS

A STEP-BY-STEP, PRACTICAL GUIDE TO USING FIFTEEN STRUCTURED COUNSELING ACTIVITIES TO IMPROVE RELATIONSHIP DYNAMICS, NEGATIVE BEHAVIOR PATTERNS, PAST WOUNDS AND EXPERIENCES, INTERNAL CONFLICTS, NEEDS AND WANTS, POWER DYNAMICS, CONNECTION AND APPRECIATION, AND DECISION-MAKING.

FOR COUNSELORS, THERAPISTS, COACHES, BEHAVIORAL HEALTH PRACTITIONERS, PROGRAM FACILITATORS, AND CONSULTANTS.

CLYDE M. FELDMAN, Ph.D.

**LICENSED MARRIAGE AND FAMILY THERAPIST
LICENSED PROFESSIONAL COUNSELOR
CERTIFIED NLP MASTER PRACTITIONER**

TUCSON, AZ
(520)-326-6060
E-MAIL: CMFELDMAN@AOL.COM
WEB: COUNSELINGTOOLSTHATWORK.COM

PREFACE

This is the **2nd Edition** (2021), with additional activities. The now **eighteen** structured activities in this guide are derived from Experiential Marriage and Family Therapy, Cognitive-Behavior Therapy, Neuro-Linguistic Programming, and Gestalt (Emotionally Focused) Therapy. <u>Six</u> of the structured activities are designed for couples and families. <u>Nine</u> are designed for solo individuals. <u>Three</u> are designed for either individuals or couples/families.

Although hundreds of structured activities for couples, families, and individuals have been developed over the last 50 years, these seventeen were specifically selected because:

- They represent a core set of structured activities which have passed the test of time in their usefulness and their potency.

- All eighteen activities are EXPERIENTIAL IN NATURE, meaning that the individual, couple, or family ENACTS SOMETHING which allows them to experience both the problem dynamic and a shift toward something more healthy. This is in contrast to simply discussing an issue and offering advice or guidance for making therapeutic changes.

- They can be used with couples, families, and individuals who have not done much counseling or therapy before. They also don't require many sessions of counseling before they can be effectively used.

- They can be applied to a wide range of presenting problems because they address very fundamental issues such as power, unexpressed needs and wants, closeness and connection, decision-making, internal conflicts, and breaking unhealthy patterns.

- The couple and family activities, specifically, always allow multiple people to participate, which gives everyone a say and incorporates all perspectives.

The structured activities described here reflect my own modifications, expansions, and enhancements over 20+ years in private practice with couples, families, and individuals.

CONTENTS

SECTION 7: RESOLVING INTERNAL CONFLICTS

SECTION 8: BREAKING NEGATIVE PATTERNS

SECTION 1:

IDENTIFYING AND UNDERSTANDING RELATIONSHIP DYNAMICS

SENTENCE COMPLETION

OVERVIEW: Sentence Completion is a structured dialogue between a couple where the practitioner presents a sentence stem and each individual completes the sentence as they see fit. It increases the ability to express core thoughts and feelings while reducing interruption, invalidation, and defensiveness. It makes overt many covert relationship dynamics and individual issues that typically remain unexpressed, out of one's awareness, or ignored.

CAUTIONS: It's important <u>not</u> to allow the couple to get into a discussion about their responses to the sentence stems. However, either partner can ask for the other to say more or to clarify something that was said. As the practitioner, don't offer your feedback and comments to the couple about what is said except to ensure that the general framework and rules are followed. After the activity is over, you can facilitate a discussion about what was said, including your own comments.

STEP 1: Have the couple sit facing each other. Explain that there are no right or wrong responses. The ground rules are:

- BOTH PARTNERS, IN TURN, COMPLETE THE SAME SENTENCE STEM, WITH ANSWERS TYPICALLY BEING A FEW SENTENCES. PARTNERS SHOULD NOT BE ALLOWED TO INTERRUPT EACH OTHER.

- PARTNERS CAN ASK CLARIFYING QUESTIONS, BUT KEEP COMMENTS AND DISCUSSION TO A MINIMUM.

- PRACTITIONER CAN ASK CLARIFYING QUESTIONS, IF NEEDED.

STEP 2: The practitioner picks some number of sentence stems to present. Which ones you select depend on your knowledge of this couple and their issues. The number presented will vary based on the time you have available. It usually takes about 45 minutes to complete them all.

STEP 3: AT THE END OF THE PROCESS, ASK EACH PARTNER:

- WHAT SURPRISED YOU MOST THAT THE OTHER PERSON SAID?

- WHAT WERE YOU HAPPIEST TO HEAR THE OTHER PERSON SAY?

- WHAT DID YOU LEARN ABOUT YOURSELF OR YOUR PARTNER IN THIS PROCESS?

SENTENCE STEMS

(listed in preferred order, but feel free to change the order)

I'm the kind of person who ____

I feel happiest when ____

Sometimes it's hard to talk about ____

A negative cycle we have is ____ -OR- A negative kind of game we play is ____

I feel insecure when ____

I feel hurt when ____

One way you help me or you are good for me is ____

You can make me feel ____ -OR- I let you make me feel ____

One way I keep myself feeling bad is ____

Sometimes I'm afraid that ____

One way I keep you distant or push you away is ____

One quality about you that I admire is ____

I feel the best / worst about myself when ____

One thing I have a hard time admitting or accepting about myself is ____

One way I've hurt you or punished you is ____

One negative way I try to get my way is ____

I need your help to ____

I get the most angry or resentful when (about) ____

One thing I can hold onto and later use against you is ____

One thing I appreciate & value the most about you, but don't often tell you, is ____

One way that I'm most like my mother or father, but don't like to admit it, is ____

One rule, or "you should-you shouldn't" statement that my mother or father always had was ____

One criticism of me I heard a lot growing up was ____

I keep expecting that ____   -OR- I keep waiting for you to ____

I need to be able to trust you to ____

I have a hard time forgiving or forgetting that ____

I need to be able to accept that ____

I don't appreciate enough ____

If we were closer ____

If you knew me better ____

One thing I wish I could change about me is ____

One way our differences compliment / conflict with each other is ____

In order to build (re-build) a healthy relationship (marriage), one of the things I might have to give up or compromise on is ____

I always hoped or imagined that a relationship (marriage) would give me ____

If I had the courage, ____

I'm not sure how to ____

I wish I could ____

The thing that I want you to understand most is ____

What I want and need most from you is ____

What I want and wish most FOR you (not from you) is ____

RELATIONSHIP SCULPTING

OVERVIEW: Relationship Sculpting offers a way to dramatize patterned relationship dynamics between a couple, within a family, or within a social system. One person assumes the role of the "sculpture" or "director" and moves and manipulates one or more other people using physical distance, gestures, and messages. Relationship sculpting makes <u>overt</u> many relationship dynamics that are <u>covert</u> or get complicated by defensiveness, blame, and over-intellectualizing. These dynamics include conflict, power and dominance, enmeshment and fusion, disengagement, alliances and coalitions, scapegoating, etc. It also provides feedback to others about what would help to change dysfunctional relationship patterns.

Sculpting is most typically used with a couple or a family. However, it can be used with a solo individual, using empty chairs to represent their partner, their family members, or others in their social system. Sculpting can be done in two phases: (1) the current view - or how things are now, and (2) the desired view - or how one wishes things would be.

CAUTIONS: First, it's important <u>not</u> to allow individuals to get into a discussion or argument about what is right or wrong, but to emphasize that this is the "sculptor's" view and what they personally experience in this relationship or family.

Second, limit the amount of in-session, between-person discussion about the "sculpture". Remember that the whole idea is to identify dynamics nonverbally and symbolically in order to bypass too much negative verbal interaction.

STEP 1: Have the person/people chose a "sculptor" or "director" to create a sculpture, picture, or portrait of how they view or see the couple/family/social relationships now in the present. Although they will be most likely be "sculpting" their partner or other family members, they can include other significant people in their social system (e.g., friends, ex-partners, etc) using empty chairs. At the end of the process, their partner and each family member should have an opportunity to become the "sculptor" and create their own picture of the couple/family relationship.

STEP 2:   Have the person chosen to be the sculptor/director identify their own position in this picture and use a chair, or some object (e.g, pillow), or the practitioner as a stand-in for that position in the room.

STEP 3:   Ask the other(s) to imagine they are like clay and their body can be moved and manipulated by the sculptor. If only one individual is present, use empty chairs to represent other people. Ask the sculptor to do the following with their partner, each family member, or each significant other in the sculpture:

- MOVE THEM TO A PLACE IN THE ROOM RELATIVE TO THE SCULPTOR'S POSITION (e.g., behind, to the side, etc.) AND AT A PARTICULAR DISTANCE FROM THE SCULPTOR'S POSITION. BE CONSCIOUS OF THE PLACE AND DISTANCE BETWEEN OTHERS, AS WELL. THIS OFTEN REPRESENTS CLOSENESS, ALLIANCES, COALITIONS, ETC.

- CHOOSE A "HEIGHT" POSITION FOR THEM RELATIVE TO THE SCULPTOR AND/OR OTHERS (i.e., higher, lower, same height) AND HAVE THEM ASSUME IT (i.e., lay down, sit, stand on a chair, etc.). THIS OFTEN REPRESENTS POWER, DOMINANCE, ETC.).

- CHOOSE A BODY POSTURE, A FACIAL EXPRESSION, OR A GESTURE THAT WOULD CHARACTERIZE OR REPRESENT THEM.

- CHOOSE SOME WORDS OR A PHRASE THE SCULPTOR WOULD ASSOCIATE WITH THEM. THIS MIGHT BE A LABEL, A CHARACTERISTIC OF THEIRS, OR A MESSAGE YOU "HEAR" FROM THEM. THE WORDS, PHRASE, OR MESSAGE CAN BE SPOKEN OUT LOUD BY THE OTHER(S) OR CAN BE WRITTEN ON A PIECE OF PAPER FOR THEM TO HOLD. (For one individual, tape the paper to the empty chair).

STEP 4:   Ask the sculptor to now put themselves into the scene by taking the position that was temporarily held by a chair, an object, or the practitioner as a stand-in.

STEP 5:   Ask the other(s) to assume their body posture or gesture, to repeat out loud their words, phrase, or message several times, or to hold up their paper with the words, phrases, or message on it.

STEP 6:   Ask the sculptor to come up with a title or caption of the whole sculpture, as if it were cast in bronze or was a painting and the title or caption was inscribed under the piece.

STEP 7:   Process the sculpture by:

ASKING THE SCULPTOR:

- WHAT DOES _____ PERSON'S POSITION, BODY POSTURE, GESTURE, AND WORD/PHRASE/MESSAGE REPRESENT, MEAN, OR FEEL LIKE TO YOU?

- WHAT DOES THE WHOLE SCULPTURE REPRESENT, MEAN, OR FEEL LIKE TO YOU? WHY DID YOU CHOOSE THAT TITLE OR CAPTION FOR IT?

- TO SAY ONE THING OF IMPORTANCE TO THEIR PARTNER, TO EACH FAMILY MEMBER, OR SIGNIFICANT OTHER. (OPTIONAL)

- TO ROLE REVERSE BRIEFLY WITH THEIR PARTNER OR ANY FAMILY MEMBER. (OPTIONAL)

ASKING THE OTHER(S):

- WHAT IS IT LIKE TO BE SCULPTED OR ARRANGED LIKE THIS?

- HOW IS THIS DIFFERENT THAN YOU THOUGHT THEY WOULD SCULPT YOU?

STEP 8:   (OPTIONAL) Have the sculptor repeat the entire process but now sculpting their <u>desired view</u> of how they wish things would be.

SECTION 2:

IDENTIFYING AND REQUESTING NEEDS AND WANTS

SATISFACTION CONTINUUM

OVERVIEW: Satisfaction Continuum provides a way to concretize the degree of relationship satisfaction or dissatisfaction where both members of a couple locate their symbolic position on an imaginary continuum from 1 to 100. It gets to the global positive and negative appraisal of the relationship while decreasing defensiveness, arguments, and repetitive details of a specific negative event. It helps couples address the seriousness of their current situation in terms of potential separation, divorce, unrealistic expectations, level of commitment, etc. it also helps couples address how one partner can contribute to increasing or decreasing the other partner's satisfaction.

While Satisfaction Continuum is most commonly used with a couple, multiple family members can have a position on the continuum.

CAUTIONS: It's important to limit the amount in-session, between-person discussion while on the line. Remember that the idea is to identify and understand the tone of the whole relationship without discussing the details of many specific events.

STEP 1: Ask each member of the couple to think about a scale from 1 to 100. 100 represents being completely satisfied, content, and happy with the relationship. 1 represents "almost" totally dissatisfied, miserable, and unhappy. 0 represents that a decision has already been made to end the relationship and a plan is in place for doing so.

STEP 2: Ask each person to imagine a line down the floor going from 1 to 100 (placing masking tape along the floor can facilitate the experience) and to move a chair to the spot along the line representing their number. Have each partner sit in their chair facing each other.

STEP 3: Initially, point out to the couple some general observations regarding the following:

- WHO'S HIGHER AND WHO'S LOWER ON THE CONTINUUM?

- WHO'S BELOW VS. ABOVE 50? (a general positive-negative mid-point)

- HOW DIFFERENT, IN RATING, ARE THEY FROM EACH OTHER?

STEP 4: Process their positions along the continuum by asking each partner the questions below (in the general order presented).

- HOW IS PERSON X'S RATING DIFFERENT THAN YOU EXPECTED?

- HOW DOES IT FEEL TO HAVE PERSON X PUT THEMSELVES AT A ___ (The other person's number)?

- HOW COME YOU'RE AT A _____ (their number) ON THE LINE?

- WHAT DOES IT FEEL LIKE TO BE AT A ___ (their number) ON THIS LINE?

- WHEN YOU THINK ABOUT YOUR WHOLE RELATIONSHIP, FROM THE BEGINNING UNTIL NOW, WHAT'S THE <u>LOWEST</u> YOU'VE EVER BEEN ON THIS LINE? WHAT'S THE <u>HIGHEST</u> YOU'VE EVER BEEN ON THIS LINE? HOW COME YOU DIDN'T STAY THERE?

- WHAT COULD PERSON X DO OR SAY THAT WOULD MOVE YOU SIGNIFICANTLY LOWER THAN WHERE YOU ARE NOW?

- WHAT COULD PERSON X DO OR SAY THAT WOULD MOVE YOU SIGNIFICANTLY HIGHER THAN WHERE YOU ARE NOW?

- WHERE DO YOU WISH YOU COULD BE ON THIS LINE IN ___ MONTHS? (e.g., 3 months, 6 months)

● WHAT'S YOUR BEST GUESS ABOUT WHERE YOU ACTUALLY WILL BE ON THIS LINE IN ___ MONTHS? (e.g., 3 months, 6 months)

EXPRESSING NEEDS AND WANTS

OVERVIEW: Expressing Needs And Wants provides a way for a couple to discuss their core issues while reducing the chance of upset and defensiveness on the part of the other partner. This is facilitated by: (1) placing the discussion in a context of being physically connected, (2) balancing what they want for themselves with what they want for the other, and (3) balancing their needs and wants with their contribution to the problems.

STEP 1:   Ask each partner to think about what they need and want in their life and in their relationship.

STEP 2:   Ask the couple to choose a way to be connected. Each partner can choose a different way to do this. Some of the most effective ways used for the purpose of this activity are:

- LAYING WITH THEIR HEAD IN THE LAP OF THE OTHER PARTNER, FACING UP.

- HUGGING.

- HOLDING BOTH HANDS.

From that position of connectedness, have the person talk about the following: (while the other mainly listens)

- WHAT DO YOU NEED AND WANT TO BE HAPPY IN YOUR LIFE?

- WHAT DO YOU NEED AND WANT TO BE HAPPY IN YOUR RELATIONSHIP?

- WHAT DO YOU WANT AND NEED FOR THE OTHER PERSON (NOT FROM THEM)?

- WHAT'S ONE WAY YOU THINK YOU CONTRIBUTE TO THE PROBLEM, TO THE NEGATIVITY, AND TO THE DISTANCE BETWEEN YOU.

STEP 3:   Switch roles and have the other partner talk about the above while remaining connected in their particular physical way.

SECTION 3:

IDENTIFYING AND UNDERSTANDING POWER DYNAMICS

PERSONAL POWER DYNAMICS

OVERVIEW: Personal Power Dynamics provides a way to symbolically represent differences in the degree of personal power experienced within a couple. It serves to make each person aware of the limitations of non-egalitarian power dynamics for both the weaker and stronger partner. It also reduces potential power struggles and increases the expression of thoughts and feelings about power dynamics because it isn't done in the context of a fight or disagreement.

STEP 1: Ask each partner to assume one of three positions:

- STANDING ABOVE THEIR PARTNER WHILE THE PARTNER KNEELS BELOW IN FRONT OF THEM.

- KNEELING DOWN IN FRONT OF THEIR PARTNER WHILE THE PARTNER STANDS ABOVE THEM.

- STANDING IN FRONT OF THEIR PARTNER WHILE PARTNER STANDS IN FRONT OF THEM.

STEP 2: From each of those positions, have them talk about the below statements and questions while the other mainly listens.

- MAKE SOME STATEMENT TO YOUR PARTNER FROM THIS POWER POSITION THAT'S "IN ROLE".

- WHAT'S IT LIKE TO BE IN THIS POSITION?

- WHAT'S GOOD/EASY AND WHAT'S BAD/HARD ABOUT BEING IN THIS POSITION?

- WHAT WOULD THE LONG-TERM CONSEQUENCES BE OF STAYING IN THIS POSITION?

- WHAT PERCENT OF THE TIME DO YOU FEEL YOU ARE IN THIS POSITION IN THE RELATIONSHIP?

- WHAT'S ONE WAY THAT YOU CONTRIBUTE TO BEING IN THIS POSITION?

- WHAT'S ONE WAY THAT YOUR PARTNER CONTRIBUTES TO YOU BEING IN THIS POSITION?

<u>YOU HAVE IT, I WANT IT</u>

<u>OVERVIEW</u>: The purpose of this activity to is re-enact typical interactional patterns and tactics during relational conflicts. This allows couples or family members to identify and explore their different conflict management styles and personal power dynamics. Simultaneously, it addresses what the most significant needs and wants are in the relationship and how the partner attempts to get them met.

While the activity is most commonly used with a couple, multiple family members can take turns in pairs.

<u>STEP 1</u>: Have the couple decide who will be partner <u>A</u> and who will be partner <u>B</u>.

<u>STEP 2</u>: Ask partner <u>A</u> to think of something that their partner has that is very important to them and that they want badly from their partner....that they need more of, don't get, or don't get enough of. This could be attention, affection, time together, help, support, understanding, etc. When they know what "it" is, have them write it on a piece of standard paper, then fold it several times to cover up what they wrote. Their job will be to get "it" anyway they can.

<u>STEP 3</u>: Give partner <u>B</u> the folded paper and tell them to put it somewhere on them, but out of sight. Tell them that their partner is going to try to get something they want from them and that "it" is written on the paper. Their job is to not let them have it under any circumstances.

<u>STEP 4</u>: Have the couple stand facing each other and give them 3-5 minutes to do their respective jobs.

<u>FOR PARTNER A</u>:

Prompt partner <u>A</u> to start by saying, "I want it", and then continue any way they can. That might include explaining why it is so important, criticizing, blaming, and guilting their partner into giving it to them, getting verbally aggressive, trying to physically get it, etc.

FOR PARTNER B:

Prompt partner B to start by saying, "you can't have it", and then continue any way they can. Do whatever is necessary to keep their partner from getting what they want and getting their way.

STEP 5:   Have the couple switch roles (partner A, B) and repeat steps 2-4.

STEP 6:   Have couples sit down and open up their respective papers and facilitate a discussion asking:

- HOW DID YOU TRY TO GET IT?

- HOW DID YOU PUT OFF THE OTHER PERSON'S ATTEMPT TO GET IT?

- HOW DID IT FEEL DOING THIS?

- IN WHAT WAYS DOES THIS REFLECT, MIRROR, OR HAVE SIMILARITIES TO THE STYLES YOU USE AT HOME?

SECTION 4:

INCREASING CONNECTION, APPRECIATION, AND UNDERSTANDING

RE-ESTABLISH A POSITIVE CONNECTION

OVERVIEW: Re-Establishing A Positive Connection provides two ways of directing a couple to experience a positive "connection" in the face of negativity. It helps a couple interrupt the spiral of negativity, whereby more and more negative messages are exchanged and fewer and fewer positive messages are exchanged. It also helps a couple be more in touch with their underlying bond and the need to operate as a team and as allies rather than enemies.

CAUTIONS: It's important **not** to force closeness, and thereby make the couple "pretend" to be getting along. The presumption is that they are in fact not getting along well, but still have some bond or positive connection that does exist and is getting lost.

DIRECT APPRECIATIONS

Ask each person to tell the other person one or more of the following: (don't have them talk to the practitioner)

- ONE THING THEY LIKE ABOUT, APPRECIATE ABOUT, OR ARE THANKFUL FOR ABOUT THE OTHER PERSON - EVEN THOUGH THINGS ARE NEGATIVE AND DIFFICULT BETWEEN THEM.

- ONE COMPLIMENT ABOUT THE OTHER PERSON RELATED TO ANYTHING THAT HAS HAPPENED IN COUNSELING TODAY OR IN COUNSELING SO FAR.

- WHAT ATTRACTED THEM TO THE PERSON IN THE FIRST PLACE?

- WHAT WERE THE BEST TIMES DURING THE FIRST 6 MONTHS OR THE FIRST YEAR THEY WERE TOGETHER?

PHYSICAL CONNECTION

Ask the couple to stand facing each other and to find some way to connect with each other physically (that might be hugging, holding hands, touching in some way, etc.) Have them stay in this position for at least 3 minutes and up to 10 minutes. During that time, ask each person to tell the other person the following: (don't have them talk to the practitioner)

- SOME STATEMENT THAT ACKNOWLEDGES THAT THEY ARE DISCONNECTED. HAVE EACH PERSON USE A STATEMENT LIKE "WE'RE NOT ACTING LIKE A TEAM", "WE'RE NOT ACTING LIKE WE'RE ON THE SAME TEAM", "WE'RE NOT TEAMING UP", "WE'RE NOT REALLY CONNECTING", "WE'RE NOT ACTING LIKE ALLIES" .

- WHAT IT'S BEEN LIKE FOR EACH PERSON TO BE DISCONNECTED. WHAT HAVE BEEN THE NEGATIVE CONSEQUENCES OR DOWNSIDE OF BEING SO DISCONNECTED.

- HOW READY OR NOT READY EACH PERSON FEELS TO RE-CONNECT. IF A PERSON IS NOT READY TO RE-CONNECT, WHAT NEEDS TO HAPPEN BEFORE THEY MIGHT BE READY.

Notice that the statements acknowledging that they are disconnected are all framed positively, in conjunction with the word **not,** rather than stated as "we're acting like <u>enemies</u>", or "we're very <u>disconnected</u>". Attempt to keep whatever each person says from being a criticism of the other.

ROLE REVERSAL AND PERSPECTIVE SHIFTING

OVERVIEW: Role Reversal (for couples and families) and Perspective Shifting (for individuals) allows a person to experience three perspectives or positions: <u>self</u> ("I", "me"), <u>other</u> ("you", them"), and <u>observer</u> ("other", "outsider"). It provides a way to: (1) improve empathy and understanding of another's views, positions, or reactions, (2) identify and understand one's own behavior and reactions within some context, and (3) better understand the broader dynamics that are taking place between two or more individuals.

When a couple or family members are present, <u>role reversal</u> allows a person to shift "positions" with another person that is actually present and gain "live" input or feedback. It often positively impacts situations where individuals: (1) are blaming and defending, (2) don't appear to understand the other's positions, why they react the way they do or did, (3) need to compromise and/or negotiate on some decision, and (4) need to better integrate or blend differing personal styles.

When only one individual is present, <u>perspective shifting</u> allows the individual to shift "positions" symbolically with another person and "see" and understand things from a different perspective. The activity can be facilitated by using empty chairs to represent significant others or by simply imagining oneself taking the perceptual positions of self, other, and observer.

ROLE REVERSAL
(a couple or family is present)

STEP 1: <u>AS YOURSELF</u> (OPTIONAL)

This step can be skipped if each person is relatively aware of their own thoughts and feelings about a problematic issue, situation, decision, or reaction AND the practitioner is relatively aware of the problems as well. If NOT, then ask each person to discuss, from their perspective, a problematic issue, situation, decision, or reaction. It's best if role reversing (step 2) takes place at a later point in time than this step.

STEP 2:   ROLE-REVERSE WITH ANOTHER PERSON:

Ask person A [Bob] to imagine that they temporarily become person B [Sue] or can step into person B's [Sue's] "shoes" or "head". Then ask person B [Sue] to image that they are person A [Bob]. Have the people physically change positions with each other and take on the other person's nonverbal or physical characteristics (e.g., sit the way they sit, talk like they talk, take their pocketbook, etc.).   As the practitioner, talk to each person as if they were, in fact, the other person. For example, call Bob "Sue" and make reference to things that recently happened to Sue (e.g., like being sick, getting really angry at Bob, etc.).

While they are in the role of the other person, ask each the following questions: (for clarification, imagine that Bob is in the role of being Sue and you are asking Bob the questions below).

- HOW ARE YOU (Sue) DOING INDIVIDUALLY / PERSONALLY?

- WHAT'S IT LIKE TO BE IN A RELATIONSHIP WITH HIM (Bob)?

- WHAT HAPPENS WHEN THINGS GO WRONG OR GO BADLY?

- WHAT DO YOU (Sue) DO OR SAY THAT KEEPS THE PROBLEM GOING OR MAKES IT WORSE?

- WHAT DOES HE (Bob) DO OR SAY THAT KEEPS THE PROBLEM GOING OR MAKES IT WORSE?

- WHAT DO YOU WANT OR WISH HE (Bob) COULD SAY OR DO DIFFERENTLY?

OPTIONALLY, while still in their role-reversed positions, you can have each person ask any questions they want of the other person during the role-reversal. This helps clarify any weakness in taking on the "other's" role and also serves to reinforce the "other's" role.

STEP 3:   BECOME THE "OBSERVER":

Have person A [Bob] and person B [Sue] each take a turn at assuming an "observer" perspective. In this "observer" role they are no longer trying to play the role of the other person, but rather, as themselves, being a neutral, more detached, outside "observer". Typically, have the person move to another physical position or another seat where they can view "the couple" [Bob & Sue] from a position "outside" of the couple. From this "observer" position, ask each:

- HOW DO YOU SEE EACH OF THESE PEOPLE [Bob & Sue].

- WHAT DO YOU SEE AS THE MAIN INTERACTIONAL DYNAMIC, PATTERN, OR THEME BETWEEN THE TWO OF THEM [Bob & Sue's dynamics].

- WHAT INPUT, GUIDANCE, OR ADVICE WOULD YOU GIVE TO EACH OF THEM [Bob & Sue] ABOUT HANDLING THE SITUATION BETTER.

STEP 4:   DEBRIEFING:

With each person back to being themselves, ask each to discuss what the role-reversal experience was like for them using the questions below as a guide:

- WHAT WAS THE EXPERIENCE OF ROLE-REVERSING LIKE FOR YOU?

- WHAT DID THE OTHER PERSON SAY THAT SURPRISED YOU OR WAS DIFFERENT THAN YOU THOUGHT?

- WHAT WOULD YOU WANT TO CLARIFY OR REINFORCE ABOUT WHAT THEY SAID WHEN THEY WERE BEING YOU?

- WHAT WAS THE MOST CHALLENGING THING ABOUT BEING THEM (the other person)?

- WHAT DO YOU HAVE A BETTER FEEL FOR, OR UNDERSTAND BETTER, AFTER BEING THEM (the other person)?

PERSPECTIVE-SHIFTING

(only one person present)

STEP 1:   TAKE THE "SELF" POSITION

Experience, describe, watch, or run a movie of a problem/conflicted issue, situation, decision, or reaction. See it through your own eyes and hearing it through your own ears. Notice your triggers, your emotional reactions, and what you are doing in your mind. Notice the other person's nonverbals and reactions, as well.

STEP 2:   TAKE THE "OTHER" POSITION

Ask the person think about another person in terms of all that they know about this other person's likes, dislikes, attitudes, background, fears, hopes, beliefs, assumptions, etc. Have them then step into the "shoes" of that person. This can be facilitated by asking them to sit in an empty chair or stand in a physical space representing the other person. From the position of being that "other" person, have them experience, describe, watch, or run a movie of the problem/conflicted issue, situation, decision, or reaction.

STEP 3:   TAKE THE "OBSERVER" POSITION

Experience, describe, watch, or run a movie of the situation from the perspective of an outside, neutral, detached observer who is seeing the situation ("they", "them") from a physical or emotional distance (e.g., projected onto a "movie" screen, hovering above it, etc.), watching both of you interact. This can be facilitated by moving to another physical chair or physical position. From this neutral position, notice and discuss:

● HOW YOU SEE YOU AND THE OTHER PERSON.

● THE INTERACTIONAL DYNAMICS BETWEEN YOU BOTH.

- WHAT INPUT, GUIDANCE, OR ADVICE YOU WOULD GIVE TO "YOURSELF" AND TO THE "OTHER" PERSON TO HANDLE THE SITUATION MORE EFFECTIVELY.

SECTION 5:

RESOLVING PAST WOUNDS AND EXPERIENCES

REFRAMING NEGATIVE LIFE EVENTS

OVERVIEW: Reframing Negative Life Events allows a person to review and re-evaluate negative life events (often a repeating pattern or cluster of events), particularly events that they attribute to their own failures, mistakes, or even bad luck. Examples of negative life events might include getting fired repeatedly, failing to follow through, having every success followed by a failure, or re-doing the same negative pattern in relationships.

STEP 1: Identify one or more (repeating pattern or cluster of) negative life events or experiences. Have the person imagine there is a "time-line" along the floor, going from "today" at one end backward to the earliest negative life event identified at the other end of the time-line (placing masking tape along the floor can facilitate the experience).

STEP 2: From the "now", have them review each event or experience by discussing the following:

- WHAT IS A WORSE SITUATION, OUTCOME, OR BEHAVIOR THAT COULD HAVE HAPPENED, BUT DIDN'T? EXPLORE THE THANKFULNESS AND GRATITUDE THAT WHAT OCCURRED WAS ONLY AS BAD AS IT WAS.

- WHAT WAS YOUR OWN AND/OR OTHER PEOPLES' POSITIVE INTENTION OR POSITIVE PURPOSE BEHIND THE NEGATIVE EVENT OR EXPERIENCE? WHAT WERE YOU TRYING TO GET, HAVE, FEEL, OR ACCOMPLISH. WHAT WERE YOU TRYING TO KEEP FROM HAPPENING OR AVOID?

- WHAT POSITIVE THINGS ULTIMATELY CAME OUT OF THE NEGATIVE EVENT OR EXPERIENCE IN SOME DIRECT OR INDIRECT CHAIN OF EVENTS. PERHAPS SOME POSITIVE THINGS WOULD NOT HAVE COME ABOUT WITHOUT THE OCCURRENCE OF THIS SEEMINGLY NEGATIVE EVENT OR EXPERIENCE.

- WHAT DID THIS EXPERIENCE TEACH YOU THAT YOU MAY HAVE NEEDED TO LEARN (i.e., life lesson), AND ARE NOW ABLE TO TAKE WITH YOU INTO THE FUTURE?

STEP 3: Go back on the time-line to the earliest event. Re-experience it again with the new reframed understanding of it. Move forward on the time-line repeating this for the other events or experiences until you have arrived at "now".

UNFINISHED BUSINESS

OVERVIEW: Unfinished Business provides a way for a person to express their unresolved feelings, unexpressed feelings, or unmet needs to another person (e.g., parent, partner, ex-partner, co-worker). The "other" person is symbolically brought into the room for the person to talk to about a wide range of experiences (e.g. abuse, negative or inconsistent behavior, betrayal, playing favorites, never setting limits, a lack of acceptance or nurturing, wanting closure to a relationship, never taking responsibility, etc.). The "Other" may be someone who the person has a current relationship with, who they used to have a relationship with, or who even may be deceased. The <u>un</u>resolved, <u>un</u>expressed, and <u>un</u>met nature of feelings and needs are often indicative of a person's inability to: (1) put them in the past, (2) put them to rest, (3) "let go" of them, (4) stop dwelling on them, or (5) get closure on them.

CAUTIONS: It's important that the person feel safe and in charge of the process and the interaction between themselves and the "Other". Therefore, ground rules related to what the "other" can't say or do, unless the person gives them permission to, are important. There is no "right" amount of time that the person should talk to the "Other". What's important is that they experience authentic intensity of emotion without suppressing what they really want to say.

STEP 1:   Have the person decide on any rules that need to be in place before talking to the "Other". The most common rule put in place is that the "Other" cannot say or do anything, but can only listen. It's important that the person feel in charge of the interaction process, given that the purpose is to express things the person has not been able to be express fully in real life.

STEP 2:   Have the person symbolically bring the "Other" into the room and have them sit or stand in a particular place in the room relative to the where the person will be. Usually, the person and "Other" are facing each other, but the "Other" could be facing away or even placed behind the person. Make sure, however, that the person can experience a clear sense of them being there in the room. Ask the person questions like: "Are they here now?", "Can you see them there?", "Can you see the expression on their face?", "Can you hear what their voice would sound like?"

STEP 3: Have the person talk to the "Other" and express their unresolved feelings and unmet needs. Encourage them to be in touch with their true emotions and true experience without avoiding, suppressing, or interrupting their flow of feelings and thoughts. During this and the remaining steps, three techniques can be used to help the person heighten their emotional awareness and fully express their core emotions: (1) ask the person to repeat what they just said 2 or 3 times (e.g., say that again; tell them again), (2) have the person repeat what they said but with more emotional intensity (e.g., try shaking your fist when you say that; say that again but angrier/louder), and (3) have the person condense, in a sentence or two, the essence of what they said over the last few minutes (e.g., "I know you had your reasons, but you were never there for me"; "you were too selfish and too drunk to pay attention to me").

DURING THIS STEP, HAVE THE PERSON:

- DIRECTLY EXPRESS THEIR CORE UNRESOLVED FEELINGS LIKE ANGER, RESENTMENT, HURT, REGRETS, DISGUST, LONGING, SADNESS, OR DISAPPOINTMENT. HAVE THE PERSON TALK TO THE "OTHER" AS "YOU", RATHER THAN "SHE", "HE", OR "THEY".

- TELL THE "OTHER" ABOUT & DESCRIBE ONE OR MORE SPECIFIC NEGATIVE EVENTS OR SITUATIONS THAT OCCURRED AND HOW THEY FEEL ABOUT EACH AND THE IMPACT EACH HAD ON THEM.

- TELL THE "OTHER" WHAT THEY WANTED, NEEDED, DESIRED, OR DESERVED, BUT DID NOT GET AND WAS MISSING.

- (OPTIONAL) IMAGE OR ENACT WHAT THE "OTHER" WOULD SAY BACK, THINK, ETC., IN ORDER TO STRENGTHEN: (1) THE PERSON'S EXPERIENCE OF THE "OTHER" BEING IN THE ROOM, AND (2) THE PERSON'S ABILITY TO RESPOND TO THE "OTHER" IN THE FACE OF THE "OTHERS'" REACTIONS.

STEP 4: Have the person tell the "Other" what they want, need, and are requesting from them <u>now</u> in order to meet the person's unmet needs, to help the person to heal, or to counterbalance things that have happened.

STEP 5: Have the person determine what needs and wants may never be fulfilled or met by this person. Then have the person talk to the "other" about:

- THE SPECIFIC UNFULFILLED, UNMET, OR UNREALISTIC EXPECTATIONS THEY HAVE AND MAY STILL CARRY AROUND, IN SPITE OF THE "OTHER'S" INABILITY OR UNWILLINGNESS TO MEET THEM. IF HELPFUL, ASK THE PERSON TO SAY THINGS LIKE: "I KEEP EXPECTING THAT ___ ", "I KEEP WANTING ___", "I KEEP HOPING THAT ___", "I KEEP TRY TO GET ___", ETC.

- THE NEGATIVE CONSEQUENCES OF HANGING ON TO THESE UNFULFILLED AND UNMET EXPECTATIONS. IF HELPFUL, YOU CAN HIGHLIGHT AND EXAGGERATE THEIR UNFULFILLED EXPECTATIONS BY ASKING THE PERSON TO SAY THINGS LIKE: "I'LL NEVER GIVE UP WANTING YOU TO MEET MY NEEDS", "I'LL KEEP TRYING TO GET YOU TO ACKNOWLEDGE WHAT YOU DID UNTIL YOU DIE".

- THE CHANGES THE PERSON WOULD LIKE TO MAKE TO THEIR UNFULFILLED AND UNMET EXPECTATIONS (e.g. Stop expecting ___ , Modify your expectations to be more realistic, Accept that the "Other" will never ___ , Disengage more from the relationship or the person, etc.).

- WHO ELSE MIGHT HELP MEET THOSE NEEDS NOW?

STEP 6: Have the person finish their "conversation" by talking about:

- WHAT THEY WANT THE "OTHER" TO UNDERSTAND MOST.

- WHAT THEY NEED TO DO OR PLAN TO DO FOR THEMSELVES.

- <u>(OPTIONAL)</u> WHAT THEY LEARNED FROM THE "OTHER" OR THEY APPRECIATE ABOUT THE "OTHER" IN SPITE OF HOW THEY FEEL.

- ANY LAST THING THEY WANT TO SAY TO OR ASK THE "OTHER" BEFORE THEY HAVE THEM LEAVE THE ROOM AND SAY GOODBYE.

CHANGING YOUR PERSONAL HISTORY

OVERVIEW: Changing Your Personal History provides a way for a person to explore negative and unhealthy reactions, interactions, emotions, attitudes, and beliefs that developed earlier in life, usually in childhood, by walking along a **past** time-line to find the earliest memory of it. Their personal history is then symbolically "changed" by having the "current-self" provide new resources to the "younger-self" that they didn't have then. The "younger-self" can then move forward in time with these new resources until they arrive at the present. This technique can be used with a wide range of issues, but a few examples might include getting too defensive, having to be right, feeling easily hurt or rejected, feeling like you're never good enough, believing that you'll never fit in or you have to be perfect or you're not allowed to "get", only "give".

CAUTIONS: It's important <u>not</u> to allow the person to over-focus on the fact that: 1) they can't remember exact details or specifics about the past (i.e., exactly what, when, who, where), 2) this situation or event may not be the earliest example of the problem pattern. Emphasize that this activity is about their <u>experience</u> of the problem at different points in their life, and that **any** early memory of it will be a powerful point of change.

STEP 1: Have the person imagine there is a time-line along the floor, starting from one end (today) and going back in time to their earliest childhood. If helpful, this can be facilitated by placing masking tape along the floor.

STEP 2: Have the person identify an unhealthy, negative, difficult, or challenging behavior, reaction, interaction, emotion, attitude, or belief to explore on the past time-line. They might think of a negative type of situation that stands out strongly in the present. They might think of a repeating negative feeling that gets in their was in the present. They might think of a limiting belief, critical inner voice, or attitude that gets in their way in the present.

STEP 3: Have the person use that negative situation or feeling or attitude/belief to identify the MOST RECENT TIME they experienced it. Have them <u>stand on the time-line</u> at that point and experience it again, as fully as possible, as if they were at that point in time now. Have them **briefly** describe, first-person, what is happening, who is involved, and the reactions, thoughts, beliefs, and feelings they are experiencing.

STEP 4: Have the person identify an even earlier time they experienced the problem situation, reaction, emotion, or attitude/belief and walk backward <u>on the time-line</u>, stopping at that point in time. Have them experience it and **briefly** describe it first-person, as if they were back at that point in time now.

STEP 5: Have the person now move backward in time <u>on the time-line</u> until they can identify the EARLIEST memory or experience of it. Once they have done that, have them imagine being that **much** younger self at that point in time. You can facilitate this leap in time by asking them questions like "how old are you?", "where do you live?" "who's in your family?", etc. Once the person appears to be in the shoes/role of that younger self, have them describe the situation and their experience of what's happening.

STEP 6: Have the person step <u>off the time-line</u> and move to an "Observer" space nearby, ideally facing where the younger self just was on the time-line. Move with the person to the "Observer" space, and say "see yourself back then/there, as if you're watching the younger "you" go through this, but you're watching as the adult you are today with all the years of experience and wisdom available to you now". Have them imagine that their younger self is still on the time-lime. From this "Observer" space, have the person spend some time identifying and discussing the following two things:

1) The <u>central or core limiting belief(s)</u> that were formed by their younger self. Ask the older self off the time-line,"What beliefs is the younger "you" (they, them) building about themselves, about other people, or about the world?" "What are they believing or generalizing about what's happening or what's being said to them?" "Was that belief only

coming from them and their experience or was it the judgement that somebody else was making or trying to put onto them?" How has that experience affected them since that time?" "What other beliefs or generalizations would they have formed as time went by?"

2) The <u>positive resources</u> that their younger self would have needed to allow them to go through this situation/experience in a better, more positive, and healthier way. Ask the older self off the time-line, "What resources do **you** have now that would have allowed the younger "you" to build a different set of beliefs back then?" "What would you have rather believed then?" "What ability, emotion, choice, or belief would you have given your younger self?" "What do you wish you could have understood, believed, felt, or done back then?"

STEP 7: From the "Observer" space, ask the person to image being able to "send" or "give" or "teach" or "transmit" any and all of those resources to their younger self who is still on the time-line. (Alternatively, you can have them "send" one resource at a time to their younger self after the person identifies each one.)

STEP 8: After all the resources have been "sent", have the person go back <u>on the time-line</u> and "step into" (the position of) their younger self and experience the event or situation, first-person, remembering that you NOW HAVE these new resources.

STEP 9: Have the person, now as their younger self, move forward in time on the time-line, taking time to stop and experience the various situations along the way, becoming aware of how things would be different now that they have the resources they needed - until they arrive at the present.

SECTION 6:

EXPLORING FUTURE DECISIONS, PATHS, AND PATTERNS

FUTURE PROJECTION

OVERVIEW: Future Projection allows a person to experience and explore an issue, problem, situation, decision, or alternative by walking along a **future** "time-line". Examples include exploring: (a) a dysfunctional emotional or behavioral pattern (e.g., substance use, depression, anxiety), (b) a job or career decision (e.g., change jobs), c) a life transition (e.g., moving, retirement), (d) the decision to move-in together, to separate, or to end a relationship, (e) life after a relationship breakup or after a loss (e.g., a death, an accident), and (f) more general issues like what "happiness" or "success" would look like in the future. Future projection helps a person become clearer about how they will likely feel, think, and react, what challenges they will likely face, and what they want to do in response. It ultimately helps a person make a better decision about choosing some path or alternative, as well as helps them better understand and manage issues and problems. During the process of walking through their "future", the person may identify and explore fears they have (e.g., of getting married, of becoming a parent, of "coming out" to their family or friends), expectations they hold (i.e., unrealistic, idealistic, "shoulds" vs. their true desires), and consequences that will likely occur (e.g., of continuing to abuse substances vs. stopping). While the technique is most commonly used with one individual, two individuals in a couple can move down side-by-side time-lines during the activity.

CAUTIONS: Keep in mind that the purpose of the activity is **not** to practice or rehearse an ideal outcome or future. But rather to take the opportunity to explore their actual thoughts, attitudes, feelings, and reactions, which may be different than the ideal or than they expect. Second, it's important <u>not</u> to allow the person to over-focus on the fact that they don't really know how things will turn out. Emphasize that this activity is about <u>imagining</u> them stepping into their future and exploring how they will likely respond, and what possible options, alternatives, or decisions they might try out.

STEP 1:   Have the person identify an issue, problem, situation, decision, or alternative they want to explore.

STEP 2:   Have the person imagine there is a time-line along the floor, starting from one end (today) and ending with some time forward (e.g., 1 year from now, 3 years from now, 20 years from now). If helpful, this can be facilitated by placing masking tape along the floor.

STEP 3:   Have the person stand (or sit if necessary) on the line at the point representing today and take one step forward at a time, first at smaller intervals (e.g., 1 month, 3 months), and then at larger intervals (e.g., 6 months, 1 year, 3 years). Make each step the person takes a clear point in time saying something like "let's move three months ahead", or "it's November 22, 2020 now", or "it's six months now since you separated." If helpful, the person can close their eyes at each stopping point. The number of steps they take along the time-line until they arrive at the end point can vary, but 6-12 stopping points is probably typical.

STEP 4:   At each stopping point on the line, check in and talk to the person in the "present", as if you are with them <u>at that point in the future</u> (i.e. "so you've been at this job for 5 fives now", "your daughter is turning 6 this month", "you broke up 3 years ago", etc). Also remember that it's ok to interject things that you, as the practitioner, are wondering about. Pay attention to and ask about holidays, anniversary dates, and birth dates as you go along the time-line. Check in by asking one or more of the questions below:

- WHAT ARE YOU DOING AT THIS POINT? WHAT'S HAPPENING AT THIS POINT (including other significant people)? HOW ARE YOU FEELING AT THIS POINT?

- WHAT'S HAPPENING WITH _____ (issue, problem, situation, decision, alternative)?

- HOW ARE YOU FEELING ABOUT _____ (issue, problem, situation, decision, alternative)?

- HOW ARE YOU HANDLING OR DEALING WITH _____ (issue, problem, situation, decision, alternative)?

- WHAT ARE YOU SURPRISED ABOUT SO FAR?

- WHAT'S HARDER, MORE DIFFICULT, OR MORE NEGATIVE THAN YOU THOUGHT IT WOULD BE? WHAT DOES THAT TELL YOU ABOUT THIS SITUATION OR YOURSELF THAT YOU NEED TO KEEP IN MIND?

- WHAT'S EASIER, GOING BETTER, OR MORE POSITIVE THAN YOU THOUGHT IT WOULD BE? ASK HOW THEY'VE BEEN ABLE TO HANDLE, DEAL WITH, COPE WITH, OR GET OVER THINGS IN A WAY THAT'S CONTRIBUTED TO IT GOING BETTER.

- WHAT'S YOUR SOCIAL SUPPORT SYSTEM LIKE AT THIS POINT?

The person can choose to try out or experiment with different options, alternatives, or actions at any point on the line (e.g., call his ex-wife, take a trip) by having them step off the line and imagine trying it out. If there are two alternatives (e.g., email vs. call; take one job vs. another, stop drinking on their own vs. go to a program), have them step off the line to the right to explore one alternative, then step off the line to the left to explore the other alternative.

STEP 5: When the person gets to the end of the time-line, have them turn around (you may want them to sit rather than stand) and look back at where they've come from. Anchor the length of time traveled by saying something like "so, it's been ____ months/years now since you were ___ (thinking about, feeling like, doing...)" or "it was ____ months/years ago when you met with ___ (practitioner), and explored the possibility/ idea of ____ . " Ask them:

- WHAT DO YOU UNDERSTAND OR ARE CLEARER ABOUT **NOW** COMPARED TO BACK THEN?

- WHAT'S YOUR ATTITUDE OR VIEW ON ____ **NOW** COMPARED TO BACK THEN?

- WHAT ARE YOU ABLE TO DO BETTER **NOW** THAN YOU WERE BACK THEN?

- WHAT WOULD YOU TELL OR ADVISE THE YOUNGER "YOU" THAT WOULD HELP THEM WITH ____ ? (issue, problem, situation, decision, alternative)

OTHER OPTIONS FOR USING FUTURE PROJECTION:

Model or Coach (addition)
Use the activity as described, but have the person identify someone who could join them on the time-line as a model or coach (at a specific point or for the entire time-line). This could be someone real or fictional, public or they know personally, living or passed away. If they're a model, this person knows how to handle this kind of situation the way they wish they could. Ask, "What are they able to do internally (attitude, beliefs, thoughts, emotions, decisions) and externally (actions, interactions) that you could try out for yourself"? If they're a coach ask, "What would they coach you to say to yourself, believe, remind yourself, picture to yourself, feel emotionally, and do in this kind of situation"? "How would they motivate you to take action or make the right decision"?

Problem/Decision Solved (alternative version)
Have the person imagine a future time-line but now projected forward to a time in their future when they have already figured out how to handle this kind of situation or have already resolved this problem or issue. Have them walk slowly along the time-line until they arrive at this point in the future. Ask them, "How did you figure this out"? "How did you resolve this"? "What are you able to say to yourself, believe, remind yourself, picture to yourself, feel emotionally, and do NOW that you weren't able to back then"? Have them turn and face their younger self at the start of the time-line and talk to them about what they understand and can do NOW that would help and guide their younger self.

Satisfactions and Regrets (alternative version)
Have the person imagine a future time-line but now projected forward to a time nearing the end of their life. It is important that they are not sick or dying but have successfully lived to the age of ___ (have them guess). Have them walk slowly along the time-line until they arrive at this point in the future. Have them turn around and "look over" their entire life from the point at the beginning of the time-line until now. Ask them, "Think about your whole life and everything that's taken place over all those years, both positive and negative. "What are the things you are most happy about, most satisfied about, and most grateful for"? Have them discuss this. Then ask them, "What are the things you regret, are most unhappy about, or are most dissatisfied with"? Have them discuss this. Then have them turn and face their younger self at the start of the time-line and offer them help and guidance on how to avoid their future regrets.

HELP FROM MENTORS

OVERVIEW: Help From Mentors is used when a person is having doubts about a decision or choice, or doubts about their purpose or mission. However, it can be useful in explo*ring a range of problematic or challenging situations. It establishes a symbolic way to get in touch with parts of oneself that know best or can provide clearer input about some decision, choice, purpose, or mission.

STEP 1:   Identify a situation in which you have doubts about some decision, choice, purpose, or mission.

STEP 2:   Identify three important "mentors" that could help to shape or influence you in a positive way by 'resonating with', 'releasing', or 'unveiling' something deeply within you. Mentors can include real people you know (e.g., friends, children, teachers), people from books, T.V., movies, history, pets and animals, and even phenomena in nature (e.g., ocean, mountains)

STEP 3:   Mark out a space or physical location (you can use chairs also) that can represent: (1) a "you" position, (2) an "observer" position, and (3) a position for each of the three "mentors" where they are around "you" in the way that seems most appropriate.

STEP 4:   From the observer position, "step" into each of the mentors, one at a time, and communicate, send, share, or state a message to the "you" who is in doubt in a way that that specific mentor would express it. The message is typically a verbal statement, but it may be sent through whatever channel is most appropriate for that mentor.

STEP 5:   Return to the observer position, and from there identify a theme that connects the three messages, or an underlying common message that connects them in some way. Once again, physically "step" into each mentor position, one at a time, and communicate, send, share, or state that common message in the way that that specific mentor would express it.

STEP 6:   "Step" into the "you" position and experience your mentors around you communicating their individual messages and then the common message. Feel the messages coming in and notice how your perception of the situation changes.

SECTION 7:

RESOLVING INTERNAL CONFLICTS

CONFLICT INTEGRATION

OVERVIEW: Conflict Integration allows a person to explore two conflicted, opposing, or struggling "parts" of themselves <u>by having the person interact with the two parts of themselves as an outside observer and facilitator</u>. In that role, the person identifies the positive purpose each part has for them and facilitates a negotiation between the parts that allows the parts to cooperate and integrate. The kinds of conflicted parts that can be explored with this technique fall into three types. They are:

1.   The common conflicted, opposing, or struggling parts, and mixed feelings that people experience (e.g., I want to ___, but I really shouldn't; I should ___, but I don't really want to; I need to be strict, but I want to be lenient; Part of me is shy, but part of me wants to be the center of attention; I want to get closer, but part of me is afraid of getting rejected so I put up a wall; I want to leave, but part of me doesn't because I'll be alone).

2.   A part of "self" that has a critical "voice" vs. a part of "self" that dislikes and is uncomfortable with that critical voice.

3.   A part of "self" that engages in a behavior that some other part of self dislikes, feels bad about, or finds objectionable (e.g., substance abuse, over-eating). The conflict integration technique can be used to help resolve the higher level conflicted motivations, incongruities in beliefs, and mixed emotions underlying the negative behavior.

STEP 1:   Have the person identify an internal conflict or struggle and put one side of the conflict symbolically in their open left palm facing up, and the other side of the conflict symbolically in their open right palm. Allow the person to decide which side to put in which palm.

STEP 2:   Have the person form a visual or mental image representing each part. The visual images could be of an object, a symbol, or it can be "seeing yourself in that position or part." Have them describe each part.

STEP 3:   Have the person ask each part (represented by the open palm facing up) what its positive intention is for them. Ask the person, "What is that part trying to give you, trying to get for you, trying to do for you, trying to have you feel, trying to accomplish for you, or trying to protect you from?" Ask two or more times in order to reach the highest level of positive intention: "If you had that, what would that give you or allow you to be, have, or do?" "What else is that part trying to give you that's even more important?"

STEP 4:   Have the person ask each part what resources (i.e.,skills, abilities, qualities) that part has and brings to the situation and to them.

STEP 5:   Say to the person: "Let that part know that you fully recognize its positive purpose and positive intention and resources, either by silently telling it or in any other way that you want to." Remind the person that they do not have to like that part's behavior, but are acknowledging and appreciating a part of them that wants __ for them and has those skills and resources.

STEP 6:   Ask the person if each part now realizes, and can appreciate, the other part's positive purpose and intention, as well as the resources that that part brings. Have each side express some appreciation for what is good or valuable about the other part saying, "I want you to watch as your two parts (i.e., palms) turn toward each other and express appreciation for the positive intention of the other part. You might hear them speaking to each other, or might see some kind of nonverbal interchange."

STEP 7:   Have the person begin a negotiation process between the parts (hands) saying, "Now I want you to look at the middle ground between your two hands...these two parts of you." "Now I want you to form a third image of what the parts would look like if they combined their resources and each part's positive purposes for you. Put that image in the center between the other two parts."

"Now, turn your palms facing each other and allow your hands to come together, only as fast as your mind can integrate these parts and allow them to cooperate and work together...keeping the positive purposes each has for you...having each part gain the resources the other brings...coming together in a way that's right for them. You may be surprised by exactly how they change and merge when your hands come together, so I want you to take all the time you need for them to merge, integrate, or blend at their own rate of speed...as your hands move together, a little or a lot, it's a signal from your unconscious mind to your conscious mind that you're changing, in ways that you may not fully understand yet."

[If the person is unable to reach the point where their hands actually come together, you can choose to handle this in one of two ways based on your knowledge of the person and their issue. First, you can consider this as fully integrated as the parts are able to become at this point, saying something like "the parts are acknowledging each other and working on a way of joining together....let that process continue in its own way and in its own time". Second, you can further facilitate this process by asking the person some additional questions as their hands are working on coming together. For example say or ask: "What does each part need to reassure the other so they can better come together?", " What does each part need the other to understand or trust so they can better come together?", "Remind each part that you need BOTH of them joining together in order to get that balance of what they have to offer you."]

STEP 8: Have the person get confirmation that the integration process has happened (e.g., physiologic changes.) and reinforce that process saying, "Keeping your hands together, slowly bring this new merged, blended, joined, or integrated part toward your chest. When your hands touch your chest, this part can join fully with you...becoming a part of your thoughts, feelings, and behaviors...now and into the future."

STEP 9: Have the person think of a specific time or situation in the past where this kind of internal conflict has occurred. Say "Imagine taking this new cooperation and joining of these parts of you - back to that situation...notice how that situation would be different now. Say "Imagine a situation in the near future where these parts of you are working together and cooperating...notice how that situation would be different."

CONFLICT SPLIT

OVERVIEW: Conflict Split allows a person to explore two conflicted, opposing, or struggling "parts" of themselves <u>by having the parts dialogue with each other</u>. The person plays the role of each opposing side and moves back and forth between parts. This dialogue process serves to highlight the underlying struggle as a self-to-self struggle. It also facilitates greater self-understanding and ultimately greater cooperation between parts. The kinds of conflicted parts that can be explored with this technique fall into three types. They are:

1.   The conflicted parts, opposing parts, or mixed feelings that people commonly experience (e.g., I want to __, but I really shouldn't; I should __, but I don't really want to; I need to be strict, but I want to be lenient; Part of me is shy, but part of me wants to be the center of attention; I want to get closer, but part of me is afraid of getting rejected so I put up a wall; I want to leave, but part of me doesn't because I'll be alone).

2.   A part of "self" that has a critical "voice" vs. a part of "self" that dislikes and is uncomfortable with that critical voice.

3.   A part of self that engages in a behavior that some other part of self dislikes, feels bad about, or finds objectionable (e.g., substance abuse, over-eating). The conflict integration technique can be used to help resolve the higher level conflicted motivations, incongruities in beliefs, and mixed emotions underlying the negative behavior.

STEP 1:   Have the person identify an internal conflict and choose one empty chair to represent one side of the conflict and another empty chair to represent the other side of the conflict. Have the chairs face each other at a distance that the person feels is appropriate. Ask the person to give each side (chair) a one word or one phrase label that would best represent that side or part.

STEP 2: Facilitate a <u>dialogue back and forth between the sides</u> by having the person sit in each chair speaking in the first person as that part, side, or position. Then have them move back and forth between chairs at times when you will prompt them to switch. Prompt the person to switch roles from one part (chair) to the other part (chair) when: (1) one part appears to have finished saying what they needed to say, and when (2) you, as the facilitator, want to know how the other part would respond to what this part just said. You can prompt the person to move to the other chair by saying: "go ahead and switch", "what do they have to say about that" (pointing to the other chair), or by just pointing to the other chair.

It's important that each part/side <u>talks directly to the other</u> part/side, rather than talking to the practitioner. Have the person begin the dialogue by sitting in the chair (side) that they are more "in touch with" or are more aware of. The dialogue has three phases which are described below. During all three phases of the dialogue, do the following:

- ACTIVELY PROMPT EACH PART TO EXPRESS ITS THOUGHTS AND FEELINGS (Example Prompts: "Tell her that", "Tell her what it's like for you" "Ask her why she doesn't trust you?", "Ask him why he can't let you be yourself?", "What do you think of the point she just made?", "What do you want to say to that side?", "Tell him about that").

- ACTIVELY PROMPT EACH PART TO RESPOND TO THINGS THE OTHER PART/SIDE SAYS (Example Prompts: "How does that make you feel?", "What do you want to say to that?", "Tell her what it's like when she says ___ ").

- ACTIVELY PROMPT EACH PART TO EXPRESS SOMETHING THAT YOU BELIEVE MAY BE TRUE FOR THAT PART, BUT IS NOT BEING SAID (Example Prompts: "Tell him that you feel alone and scared", "Tell them how much of a disappointment you are to them").

- ACTIVELY PROMPT EACH PART TO EMPHASIZE AND REPEAT IMPORTANT STATEMENTS THAT IT MAKES (Example Prompts: "Say that again", "Say that even stronger").

- ENCOURAGE EACH PART TO STAY WITH THEIR FEELINGS INSTEAD OF STRUGGLING OR DEFENDING AGAINST THEM OR SUPPRESSING THEM IN ORDER TO HELP THEM EXPERIENCE THEIR CORE FEELINGS (i.e., sadness, despair, insecurity, inadequacy, exhaustion) (e.g., "I feel defeated", "I'm afraid life is passing me by", "I feel all alone", "I think I'm worthless) (Example Prompts: "What are you feeling as she says you're___ ?", "Stay with the sadness", "Stay with those feelings").

PHASE 1 OF THE DIALOGUE:

This first phase of the dialogue highlights the conflict dynamics. Ask each side to talk to the other side about:

- WHO THEY ARE. (Example Prompts: "How would you describe yourself?", "Tell them who you are", "Tell them what you're like")

- HOW THEY VIEW, FEEL ABOUT, AND THINK ABOUT THE OTHER PART/SIDE. (Example Prompts: "Tell them how you feel about them", "Tell them what you think of them")

- THE NEGATIVE TACTICS THE OTHER PART/SIDE USES ON THEM TO MAKE THEM FEEL BAD OR TO GET THEM TO DO WHAT THEY WANT. ALSO HOW THESE TACTICS MAKE THEM FEEL. (e.g., guilts them, criticizes and belittles them, acts superior, etc.) (For Example: How does one side exacerbate, scare, or criticize the other side? How does one side assume the other side doesn't know how to do things or isn't good enough? How does one side make the other side actually feel worse, feel depressed, hopeless, anxious, insecure or unsure - and have to defend itself, or make excuses?) (Example Prompts: "Are you aware of how you're scolding that side?", "Try to make her afraid right now", "Tell them how insecure you feel when they try to ___ ")

- THEIR CRITICISMS, DISLIKES, UPSETS, AND NEGATIVES ABOUT THE OTHER PART/SIDE. (Example Prompts: "Tell him what you expect from him", "Tell him what he should do", "Be more specific about what you don't like")

- WHAT THEY WANT AND NEED FOR THEMSELVES.

PHASE 2 OF THE DIALOGUE:

The second phase of the dialogue focuses on identifying the positive intentions and purposes each side has, in spite of their negative style or tactics. Ask each side to talk to the other side about:

- THEIR POSITIVE INTENTION OR POSITIVE PURPOSE BEHIND TAKING THIS POSITION OR DOING WHAT THEY DO. ASK: "WHAT ARE YOU TRYING TO GIVE THEM, TO GET FOR THEM, TO DO FOR THEM, TO ACCOMPLISH FOR THEM, TO PROTECT THEM FROM, OR TO HAVE THEM FEEL?" (e.g., "I'm afraid you'll make the same mistake as before", "I feel really protective of you", "I don't want you to get hurt", "I want you to make good decisions so I'm watching out for you, "I'm trying to get you motivated", "I'm trying to help you relax").

PHASE 3 OF THE DIALOGUE:

The last phase of the dialogue attempts to increase cooperation and integration of the two sides. Ask each side to talk to the other side about:

- WHAT THEY NEED AND WANT FROM THE OTHER PART (e.g., "Let me breath...don't stifle me", "I want you to listen to me more and not ignore me", "I want you to trust me more").

- POSSIBLE NEW WAYS TO COOPERATE AND COMPROMISE SO THAT BOTH SIDES COULD (1) ACCOMPLISH THEIR RESPECTIVE POSITIVE PURPOSE, (2) ADDRESS WHAT THE OTHER SIDE NEEDS THEM TO DO DIFFERENTLY, AND (3) USE THEIR DIFFERENCES TO COMPLEMENT EACH OTHER RATHER THAN TO WORK AGAINST EACH OTHER.

SECTION 8:

BREAKING NEGATIVE PATTERNS

CHAINING RESOURCE STATES

OVERVIEW: Chaining Resource States allows a person to develop new and more resourceful ways of thinking, feeling, and acting (desired state) in situations that are problematic or challenging now (problem state). A wide range of problems can be used with this technique, including stress, anger, depression, anxiety, rejection, self-worth, emotional over-reactions, etc. Since breaking old patterns is one of the most difficult things to do, Chaining Resource States helps a person "bridge the gap" between what they do now (problem state) and what they wish they could do (desired state) by establishing two intermediate steps (states) that the person can use. Building and practicing the sequence of going from problem state (location 1), to first intermediate state (location 2), to second intermediate state (location 3), and finally to the desired state (location 4) is done by choosing four physical locations in the room, usually in some sort of a line. A person can then either move to each location standing, or use four different empty chairs to sit in.

STEP 1: PROBLEM STATE (LOCATION 1): Identify a problem situation or problematic thinking, feeling, or acting. Choose a physical location in the room that could represent this PROBLEM STATE. Have the person move to that chair or physical spot and EXPERIENCE AND ENACT what they typically feel, say, picture to themselves, and do in this problem state.

STEP 2: DESIRED STATE (LOCATION 4): Identify a new, more resourceful way of thinking, feeling, or acting in this type of situation. Choose a physical location in the room that could represent this DESIRED STATE. Choose a location that leaves room for the two intermediate locations to come. Have the person move to that chair or physical spot and ask them: "How do you wish you could be in this situation?" What do you want to be able to do, or feel, think to yourself, picture, remind yourself, or believe in this kind of situation?" Have the person DESCRIBE this imagined, desired state. Don't expect the person to be able to ENACT AND EXPERIENCE this desired state yet.

You can use FOUR DIFFERENT METHODS to help the person develop new ways of thinking, feeling, and acting that will be resources for them in this type of situation. They are:

PAST EXPERIENCE   Remember, think of, or find a time in the past, in a similar kind of situation, when you were able to handle things more like you want to now...even if you were only able to accomplish some of what you're wanting to now. Remember that now and put yourself back into that situation now. What were you able to say to yourself, believe, remind yourself, picture to yourself, feel emotionally, and do that would help you now?

FUTURE PROJECTION   Imagine it's some time (____ months/years) in the future when you have already figured out how to handle this kind of situation or resolved this issue. Put yourself into the future. What are you able to say to yourself, believe, remind yourself, picture to yourself, feel emotionally, and do in this future time that would help you in the present?

MAGIC WAND   Imagine you had a magic wand and you could use it to (or are magically given the ability to) handle this situation that way you want to. What would it give you the ability to say to yourself, believe, remind yourself, picture to yourself, feel emotionally, and do in this kind of situation?

MODEL OR COACH   Think about someone else - real or fictional, public or you know personally, living or passed away - who knows how to handle this kind of situation the way you wish you could. What would they coach you to say to yourself, believe, remind yourself, picture to yourself, feel emotionally, and do in this kind of situation? What would they be able to do that you could try out for yourself?

STEP 3: FIRST INTERMEDIATE STATE (LOCATION 2): Choose another location (typically in-between the problem and desired locations) which could represent a FIRST intermediate step that could help the person bridge the gap from the PROBLEM STATE to the DESIRED STATE. This intermediate first step would allow them to move away from, "loosen up", or reduce the intensity of, the problem state. Have the person move to that chair or physical spot and help them first identify, and then ENACT AND EXPERIENCE what they would need to do, feel, say to themselves, picture, or believe that would help them begin to move a little farther away from the problem state and get a little closer to the desired state. You might also identify the positive purpose or intention behind the problem state as a guide to the intermediate state(s).

STEP 4: SECOND INTERMEDIATE STATE (LOCATION 3): Choose another location (typically in-between the first intermediate state and the desired state) which could represent a SECOND intermediate step that would get them even closer to being able to be the person in the DESIRED STATE. Have the person move to that chair or physical spot and first identify, and then ENACT AND EXPERIENCE the actions, feelings, thoughts, pictures, and beliefs.

STEP 5: DESIRED STATE (LOCATION 4): Have the person move to the DESIRED STATE location again and have them now ENACT AND EXPERIENCE, as best they are able to, the DESIRED feelings, self-talk, mental images, beliefs, attitudes, and behavior associated with this more resourceful state.

STEP 6: HAVE THE PERSON MOVE THROUGH THE FOUR LOCATIONS (problem → first intermediate → second intermediate, → desired) several times in sequence, stopping at each position to experience the thoughts, feelings, and actions associated with each location. After each sequence, have the person clear their mind and think about or talk about something else for 15+ seconds. Have the person identify a different word, phrase, gesture, or image for each location that could represent or symbolize it. (Some examples: saying the words "the big picture" to themselves; making the gesture of putting their hand over their heart; seeing a mental image of them comforting their younger self; remembering the time they got an award). Each time they repeat the sequence: (1) have them move through it a little more quickly, (2) when they're in the PROBLEM STATE, remind them "You can leave the problem chair/spot as soon as you're able to move out of it", and (3) have them enact the word, phrase, gesture, or image out loud or silently to themselves as they step into that location.

STEP 7: (OPTIONAL). Have the person think of a situation that will come up in the near future where they want to practice this desired state. Have them see themselves, or run a movie of themselves, using these new resources in this situation. Then have them step into the situation, in first-person, and experience using these new resources in this situation.

UPDATING NEGATIVE MESSAGES AND BELIEFS

OVERVIEW: Updating Negative Messages And Beliefs helps a person to change and "update" their negative self-talk, negative internal messages, negative inner "voice", or limiting beliefs about themselves and their world. Many times negative internal messages and beliefs were more functional or "made more sense" at the time they were originally formed. Now they no longer need to serve that original purpose (i.e., that person is gone or that situation has long since changed) or have become increasing debilitating over time (i.e., repeated self-criticism, depressing). The technique is most effective with negative self-talk or beliefs related to self-worth and adequacy, trust, success and failure, perfectionism, sense of personal power, the need for love, the need for approval, etc. The process of changing and "updating" is facilitated by helping the person to: (1) get some "distance" from the internal message and view it more as an objective observer would, (2) identify the positive purpose or intention behind it, and (3) construct a new, "updated" message that is more positive and healthy.

Internal messages and beliefs (self-talk, inner "voice") typically originate in one or two ways: (1) a person may have internalized the negative message or belief that they heard, or came, from another person directly (e.g., parent), or (2) a person may have developed their own negative message or belief based on their own experiences and reactions to circumstances. The steps to follow below are somewhat different depending on which is more true.

CAUTIONS: This technique is less effective when the negative self-talk and beliefs are clearly associated with anxiety and trauma problems (e.g., generalized anxiety, PTSD), or are clearly associated with domestic violence and anger problems. In these situations, it's probably more effective to use other techniques. For example, exposure therapy or E.M.D.R. for anxiety problems and power/control/responsibility techniques for domestic-violence and anger problems.

STEP 1: Help the person identify their specific negative self-statement, negative inner message, or limiting belief. Have the person determine if this is an internalized message/voice of ANOTHER PERSON or this is THEIR OWN message/voice. Often when it's internalized from another person, the message will use "you" rather than "I" (e.g., "you're so stupid" vs. "I'm so stupid"). Based on this, you'll choose which set of steps to use below, beginning with step 4. If it's not clear, or if it's some combination of both self and other, use the steps under "If the message/belief is their own".

STEP 2: Have the person choose a location in the room that can represent a "Message/voice" space, where they can be in touch with what their inner message, voice, or belief is "saying" or "telling them" and have them go and stand or sit in that place. Then have the person re-experience or "hear" that message/voice. It can be helpful to have them think of a problem time or problem situation that the inner message/voice is often associated with. Have them also notice its tone (loud, soft, sarcastic, critical, etc.) and where it appears to be located or coming from. Commonly, we experience the message/voice as being located outside of us, somewhere around our head. And even if it's experienced as being inside our head, it's not coming from our actual throat or mouth.

STEP 3: From the "Message/voice" space, have the person choose another place in the room that can represent an "Observer" space, where they can be temporarily "free" of the message/voice/belief and where they could think about it and evaluate it from a more neutral, "outside observer" perspective. Ask the person to imagine that you're able to physically hold on to their message/voice and keep it in place, while they walk away from the "Message/voice" space and go to the "Observer" space. Have them go and stand or sit in that place.

IF THE MESSAGE/VOICE IS INTERNALIZED FROM ANOTHER:

STEP 4:   From the "Observer" space, determine who the other person is that's associated with the message/voice/belief and have the person imagine bringing them symbolically into the "Message/voice" space along with the negative message/voice itself. Then identify the positive intention(s) or purpose(s) that this person may have had (or the message has). Ask, "What were they (is it) trying to give, get, or do for you?" "What were they (is it) trying to protect you from or help you avoid?". Help the person make a clear distinction between the person's (its) POSITIVE INTENTION, in contrast to the person's (its) NEGATIVE WAY of trying to accomplish that purpose.

STEP 5:   From the "Observer" space, have the person identify the resources the other person would have needed to provide a better and different message/voice that accomplishes the same positive intention and purpose. Resources might be related to the other person's attitude, actions, emotions, lifestyle, etc. and could be skills, abilities, qualities, or choices the person would have wanted or needed them to have. Then have the person imagine giving, transmitting, or sending those "symbolic" resources to the other person.

STEP 6:   From the "Observer" space, have the person identify a better, healthier, more helpful message/voice that is able to accomplish that same positive intention and purpose in a new and better way, based upon how the other person and their message would change now that they have the new resources. The change is often both in the CONTENT of the message and in its TONE (e.g., softer, kinder, nicer, more understanding). Have the person "ask" or determine if the old message/voice is open to an a new and better way to accomplish its positive intention (i.e., to being updated). If it is, have the person imagine giving, transmitting, teaching, or sending the new, updated message to the old one (or to the person if appropriate). If it's NOT open, help the person determine what would help it be more open and help the person work to get a "YES", even if it's a partial or conditional "YES".

STEP 7: From the "Observer" space, have the person ask or allow the other person in the "Message/voice" space to leave. Help the person to realize and acknowledge that this message/voice has become theirs and is a part of them. Once the other person is "gone", have the person leave the "Observer" space and go back to the "Message/voice" space and step back into the position they were standing/sitting in originally (in step 2). Have them now "try on", hear, and experience the new, changed, updated message/voice fully. Make any other changes to the content or tone that are needed.

IF THE MESSAGE/VOICE IS THEIR OWN:

STEP 4: From the "Observer" space, identify the positive intention(s) or purpose(s) that this negative message/voice may have. Ask, "What is it trying to give, get, or do for you?" "What is it trying to protect you from or help you avoid?" Help the person realize that they created, and are holding on to, this message/voice for a positive reason or purpose. Help them make a clear distinction between its POSITIVE INTENTION and what it wants for them, in contrast to its NEGATIVE WAY of trying to accomplish that purpose for them. To reinforce this point, have the person give direct appreciations and thanks to the message/voice for its positive intention and purpose, separate from its negative style.

STEP 5: From the "Observer" space, have the person identify a better, healthier, more helpful message/voice that is able to accomplish the same positive intention but in a new and better way. The change is often in both the CONTENT of the message and in its TONE (e.g., softer, kinder, nicer, more understanding). Have the person "ask" or determine if the old message/voice is open to a new and better way to accomplish its positive intention (i.e., to being updated). If it is, have the person imagine giving, transmitting, teaching, or sending the new, updated message to the old one. If it's NOT open, help the person determine what would help the old message/voice be more open and help the person work to get a "YES", even if it's a partial or conditional "YES".

STEP 6:   Have the person leave the "Observer" space and go back to the "Message/voice" space and step into the position they were standing/sitting in originally (in step 2). Have them now "try on", hear, and experience the new, changed, updated message/voice fully. Make any other changes to the content or tone that are needed.

DISRUPTING THE NEGATIVE IMPACT OF MENTAL PICTURES AND IMAGES

OVERVIEW: This is a set of related techniques designed to help disrupt, interrupt, and reduce the potency of what a person "sees" internally in their mind's eye as mental PICTURES, IMAGES, and MOVIES. While most people are aware of their self-talk and internal dialogue, they are often unaware of the mental images that they make in a range of situations and circumstances. In fact "thinking", at its most fundamental, is "encoded" as self-talk and mental pictures and movies. These internal images are associated with remembering past events, creating future expectations, interpreting ongoing events, perceptions of others, self-image, and core beliefs and attitudes we hold about ourselves, others, and the world. This set of techniques is effective for a wide range of negative reactions and negative emotional states, particularly in situations where people say "I get triggered", "I'm really sensitive", or "I over-reacted". Some examples include being overly - frustrated, irritated, defensive, anxious, impatient, hurt, or being sensitive to criticism, rejection, etc.

The power of this set of techniques lies in understanding that all internal images, pictures, and movies we make have specific characteristics or qualities, separate from their actual content. For example, remembering you and your best friend talking at dinner might be "seen" in your mind's eye as a color (instead of B&W) snapshot (instead of a movie) viewed from an observer position of the two of you talking (instead of viewed first-person) appearing about a foot in front of your head (instead of 3 feet) and up to your right (instead of down to your left). These characteristics of mental pictures are important because it is often what allows the information to carry so much emotional weight or intensity, both positive (e.g., appreciative, relaxed) and negative (e.g., anxious, angry). These techniques modify those qualities so the images have less negative intensity and negative impact and ultimately allow the person to being to develop more positive and resourceful images. An example is:

A woman often feels afraid and gets "triggered" when she has disagreements with her boyfriend. During the disagreements, she became aware that she was picturing a former boyfriend who was verbally abusive to her in similar situations. Her picture of him is large in size, close in, and bright. By asking her to practice "zooming out" that image, it became smaller and dimmer, with far less emotional potency. The interactions with her boyfriend became far less "triggered" and sensitive.

THE 12 MOST COMMON QUALITIES AND CHARACTERISTICS THAT ARE THE FOCUS OF CHANGE:

(You might try remembering a negative interaction between yourself and another person to better understand the items below).

1. <u>The viewer's orientation</u>. Is your view or perspective as though you're looking out of your own eyes seeing the other person and the surrounding (1st person)? Is your view or perspective as though you're seeing you and the other person arguing (3rd person)?

2. <u>The type of mental image</u>. Is it a still picture, like a snapshot, a series of still images, or a movie?

3. <u>The location of the mental image in your visual field</u>. Where do you get a sense that the image or movie is located or coming from? Where do you see it outside of your head? Typically we "see" mental images in front of us, often upper left, upper right, lower left, or lower right. However, we might "see" it to the side or fairly centered in front of us.

4. <u>The distance of the mental image from you</u>. How far away does the image or movie appear to be? This can be fairly close (i.e., inches away) or farther (i.e. feet away).

5. <u>The size of mental image</u>. How big does the image or movie appear to be?

6. <u>The color of the mental image</u>. Is the image or movie in B&W or color?

7. <u>The brightness of the mental image</u>. How bright vs. dim does the image or movie appear to be?

8. <u>The focus or clarity of the mental image</u>. How clear and in-focus vs. unclear and out-of-focus does the image or movie appear to be?

9. <u>The depth quality of the mental image</u>. How flat and 2D vs. how deep and 3D does the image or movie appear to be?

10. <u>The sound/voices associated with the mental image</u>. Does the image or movie have sound/a soundtrack or is it silent? If yes, what kinds of sounds (voices, nature sounds, music, etc.)?

11. <u>The volume and tone of the voices/sounds associated with the mental image</u> How loud vs. soft are the sounds? What's the tone of the voices/sounds (angry, friendly, sarcastic, critical, serious, playful, etc.)?

12. <u>The distance and location of the voices/sounds</u>. How far away vs. close do the voices/sounds seem? Do they seem to come from the same location as the image or from another location?

<u>STEP 1:</u> Identify the specific mental picture or movie that is elicited when the person has an overly intense or overly negative emotional, behavioral, or attitudinal reaction in some problem situation. To facilitate this, have the person briefly re-experience, remember, or put themselves back in the negative situation or negative reaction and ask them to notice any internal images they're making or are coming up. You might ask them: (1) "When you start to feel or react this way, what do you see in your mind's eye?", (2) "Put yourself back in that situation now and notice what's going through your mind and what mental pictures or movies you're making?", (3) "Imagine this is happening again and you can experience it right now, what are you remembering or picturing about the past?", and (4) "Imagine this is happening again and you can experience it right now, what are you imagining or picturing about the future?"

STEP 2: Help the person describe as many of the qualities or characteristics (listed above) of the image, picture, or movie as possible.

STEP 3: Use the one or more of the techniques below to change the qualitites or characteristics of the image, picture, or movie in order to disrupt it, interrupt it, or reduce its potency. For most qualities and most people, the change is in a pre-defined direction (e.g., smaller, dimmer, farther away, lower volume, less harsh, etc.). However, for some qualities (location in the visual field, filter, framing, tone) the change isn't pre-defined and will be different for different people. Also, some people do not fit the norm, so experimenting with what to change about the quality is useful. It can be very helpful for the person to imagine that they have a remote control and can use it like they would with their T.V. or DVD.

- Change the image/movie from 1ˢᵗ person to 3ʳᵈ person, or view it from hovering above.

- Move or "zoom" the image/movie farther out, farther away. It can be moved so far away that it can hardly been seen, or is the size of a postage stamp, or moves out all the way to the horizon.

- Make the image/movie smaller.

- Move the image/movie to a different location in the visual field (e.g., higher up, lower down, more to the left, to the one's right side, etc.).

- Make the image/movie B&W if its in color.

- Make the image/movie dimmer.

- Make the image/movie more out-of-focus or more 2D.

- Switch or turn the image/movie off (like turning off the T.V.).

- Change the image from a movie to a still photo/snapshot.

- Put the movie on pause.

- Run the movie backward as if you had a remote control and you pressed reverse (slow, med, or fast).

- Make the image/movie have a filter on it to change its color, brightness, etc.

- Change the relative position or size of people and things in the image/movie (e.g. make yourself 100' tall; shrink others down).

- Put the image/movie in a "container" (a box, a safe, a closet, a cave, etc.) or send it or put it away where it cannot return.

- Place a protective shield or glass wall around you or between you and the image/movie.

- Disrupt the image/movie by seeing it as made of glass, painted on glass (window), or seen in a mirror. Then shatter it into a thousand pieces.

- Disrupt the image/movie by seeing it on the surface of water (pond, swimming pool, etc.). Then throw a stone in it, or imagine a windstorm or rainstorm disrupting the surface.

- Disrupt the image/movie by seeing it as a painting. Then imagine using water or some other liquid to make it run.

- See the image/movie as film where the projection lamp burns a hole in, or melts, each frame.

- See the image with a distinct frame around it. Apply a frame that allows the image to feel more adaptive/neutral such as a large, baroque frame, an old time oval frame, a colored plastic frame, etc.

- Turn the voices/sounds off ("mute it) or turn down the volume.

- Make the voices/sounds slow down or speed up.

- Make the voices/sounds change in tone so that they sound distorted, or ridiculous, or like cartoon character voices.